MY FIRST ENCYCLOPEDIA

An eye-catching series of information books designed to encourage young children to find out more about the world around them. Each one is carefully prepared by a subject specialist with the help of experienced writers and educational advisers.

KINGFISHER

Kingfisher Publications Plc

New Penderel House, 283-288 High Holborn, London WC1V 7HZ

First published in paperback by Kingfisher Publications Plc 1994

2 4 6 8 10 9 7 5 3 1

1BP/0500/SF/(FR)/135MA

Originally published in hardback under the series title Young World

This edition © copyright Kingfisher Publications Plc 2000

Text & Illustrations © copyright Kingfisher Publications Plc 1992

ISBN 1 85697 262 3

Phototypeset by Waveney Typesetters, Norwich

Printed in China

On the Move

Kingfisher

Series consultant and author
Brian Williams

Educational consultant
Daphne Ingram

Editor
Sian Hardy

Designer
Robert Wheeler

Illustrators
Peter Dennis (pages 12-13, 52-53, 96-97)
Andrew French (pages 66-67, 70-71, 74-75)
Tony Gibbons and Lawrie Taylor (pages 64-65, 68-69,
72, 80-81, 92-93 *bottom*, 100-101)
David McAllister (pages 82-83, 86-87, 90-91, 92-93 *top*)
Industrial Art (pages 78-79)
Oxford Illustrators (pages 14-17, 22-23, 26-27, 34-35,
38-41, 44-49, 54-59, 73, 98-99, 102-119)
Vincent Wakerley (pages 20-21, 24-25, 28-31,
36-37, 42-43, 50-51, 84-85, 88-89)

About this book

Whenever you catch a bus or a plane, ride in a car or on a bicycle, you are using a form of transport.

Transport means carrying things and people from place to place. Early forms of transport were slow. Today, journeys that used to take days, or even weeks, take only a few hours. A jet aeroplane can fly around the world in just one and a half days.

Because transport has become faster, easier and cheaper, our world and the way we live have changed. Our cities have airports. Roads, tunnels and bridges criss-cross the countryside. People often travel to faraway places, and our shops are filled with goods from all over the world. We depend on transport.

People around the world travel in many different ways. In some countries people drive on the right-hand side of the road. In others they drive on the left. In this book we have shown a mixture of left- and right-hand drive, as well as a selection of number plates from different countries.

CONTENTS

ALL KINDS OF TRANSPORT

WHEELING ALONG

FOUR WHEELS MORE WHEELS

WHEELS ON RAILS

OCEAN TRANSPORT

INTO THE AIR

THE SPACE AGE

All kinds of

transport

 A busy street

This busy street is full of people on the move. A truck delivers fish that has come from far away to a fishmonger. A bus takes people to work or school. All around us are cars, trucks and motorbikes carrying people and things from one place to another.

✹ Around the world

So much of the food we eat every day comes from faraway places. Have you ever thought how it reaches us?

Roads and railways join cities that are hundreds of kilometres apart. Big container ships bring us food from countries across the sea.

Planes travel faster than ships or trains or trucks. A big jet can fly around the world in only one and a half days. Some planes carry cargo, but most are used to carry passengers. Rockets can now even carry people into Space.

✷ Animal power

People cannot always use cars and trains to move around. In some places it would be too difficult to build a road or a railway.

Camels can walk for days across a hot desert. Most cars would sink into the sand. In the jungle, the easiest way to get around is often to take a canoe down the river.

When this happens, people often use animals to help them carry their heavy loads from place to place.

High up in the mountains of Peru, people use llamas to carry their loads. In Lapland, the Lapps use reindeer to pull their sledges across the snowy ground.

Amazing facts

✸ The wheel was the first important transport invention. People first made wheels over 5,000 years ago. They made them by fastening pieces of wood together.

✸ The world's longest highway is the Pan-American Highway. It is over 24,000 kilometres long, although there is a gap in the middle. It starts in Alaska in the far north of North America and ends in Brazil in South America.

✸ The biggest car park in the world is in Edmonton, in Canada. It has parking spaces for 30,000 cars.

Wheeling

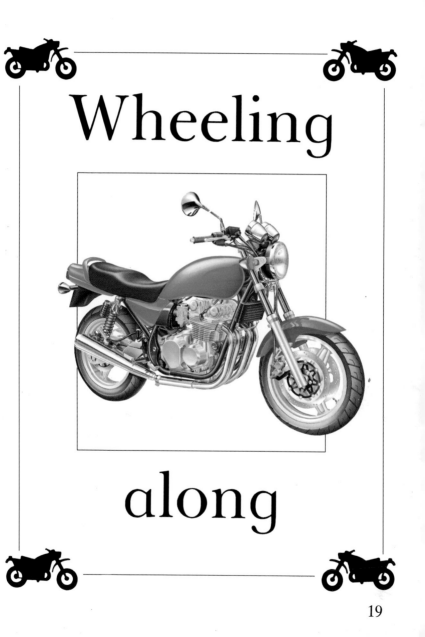

along

🏍 A bicycle

On a bicycle you use your feet to move the pedals. Follow the numbers to find out what happens next.

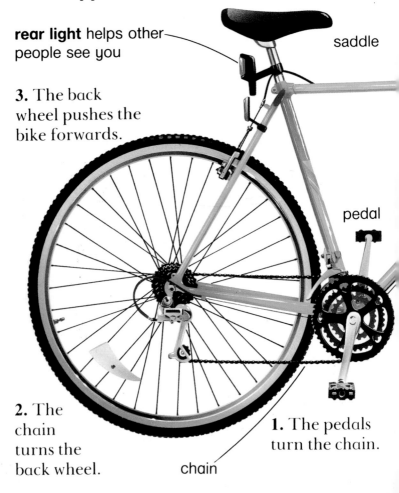

rear light helps other people see you

saddle

3. The back wheel pushes the bike forwards.

pedal

2. The chain turns the back wheel.

1. The pedals turn the chain.

chain

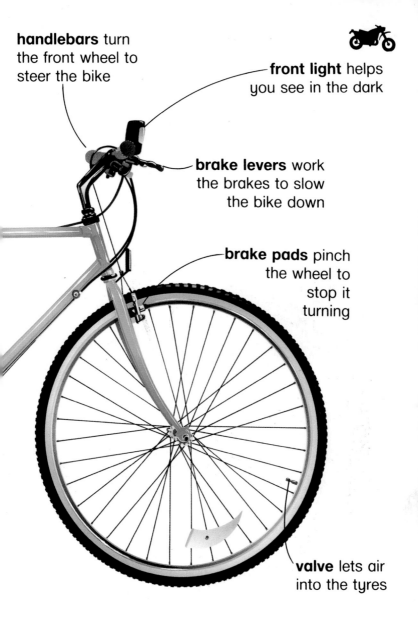

handlebars turn the front wheel to steer the bike

front light helps you see in the dark

brake levers work the brakes to slow the bike down

brake pads pinch the wheel to stop it turning

valve lets air into the tyres

21

🏍️ Safety on a bike

Riding a bike is fun, but always remember:
safety first! Check your bike regularly and
take it to a repair shop if anything is wrong.
You should learn your highway code before
cycling on the road. The picture shows you
eight things you need for your bike.

1 pump

2 light

3 reflector bands

4 oil can

5 puncture repair kit

6 helmet

7 bell

8 tool kit

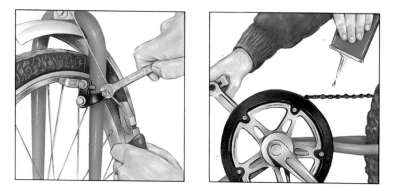

Make sure the brake pads have not worn down and always keep your chain well oiled.

You may need help to mend a puncture. First find the hole in the inner tube, and then cover it with a patch.

🏍 Early bikes

People have enjoyed riding on two wheels ever since bicycles were first invented.

The hobbyhorse was an early bike with no pedals. You pushed yourself along with your feet.

Later bikes, like the vélocipède, had pedals fixed to the front wheel.

Because of its big front wheel, the penny-farthing could go very fast. But it was difficult to ride.

One, two, three wheels

A one-wheeled cycle is called a unicycle, and a three-wheeled cycle is called a tricycle.

Could you balance on a unicycle?

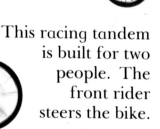

This racing tandem is built for two people. The front rider steers the bike.

In some Asian cities, pedal-powered rickshaws are used as taxis.

🏍 A motorbike

A motorbike is powered by a petrol engine. The engine drives a shaft or a chain that turns the back wheel. The back wheel pushes the motorbike forwards.

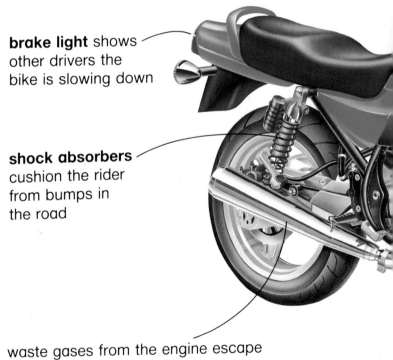

brake light shows other drivers the bike is slowing down

shock absorbers cushion the rider from bumps in the road

waste gases from the engine escape through the **exhaust pipe**

mirror

brake lever

speedometer shows how fast the bike is going

tank holds petrol to fuel the engine

headlight

indicator

petrol engine

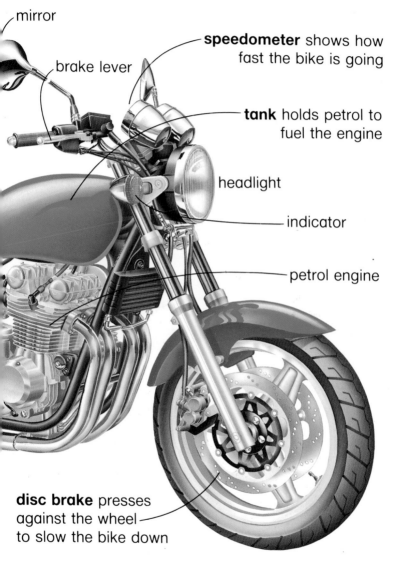

disc brake presses against the wheel to slow the bike down

🏍 Working bikes

The police use fast motorbikes. Unlike cars, which need lots more space, motorbikes are not held up in traffic jams. So a police motorcyclist can quickly reach an accident and call for help by radio.

🏍 All kinds of bikes

Mopeds have smaller engines than motorbikes and so are less powerful.

The Harley Davidson is a powerful American motorbike. Its engine is bigger than the engine of a small car.

A sidecar fixed to the side of a motorbike can carry an extra passenger.

🏍️ Racing bikes

People enjoy racing pedal bikes and motorbikes. They race on tracks and on roads. Racers use bikes that are faster than ordinary bikes.

The Tour de France is the most famous pedal bike race. The race is in stages and lasts about three weeks.

In motocross races, riders scramble their bikes over bumps and through streams.

Drag bikes only race along a short track, but they reach speeds of over 300 kilometres an hour in a few seconds.

Grand Prix racers speed around a winding track. The riders lean into the bends to keep their balance.

Amazing facts

Air-filled bicycle tyres were invented by John Dunlop about 60 years after the first bicycle appeared. Before that, bicycle wheels had metal or wooden rims. This made them very uncomfortable to ride.

The Tour de France is the longest bicycle road race. It covers more than 3,000 kilometres in total, but is broken into stages.

The fastest speed on a motorbike is over 512 kilometres an hour. This record was set by Donald A. Vesco in 1978 on a bike with two engines.

A 'wheelie' means riding on the back wheel only. The record for a wheelie on a motorbike is an amazing 331 kilometres non-stop.

Four wheels

more wheels

 # A car

A car has hundreds of parts. It has a strong metal frame, called a chassis, and a body made of thin metal panels. Follow the numbers to see how it works.

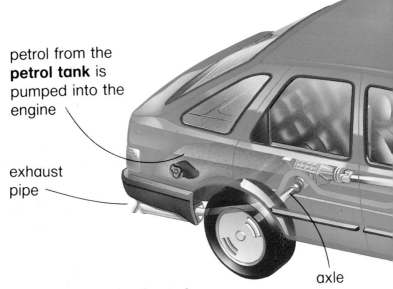

petrol from the **petrol tank** is pumped into the engine

exhaust pipe

axle

5. The back wheels push the car forwards. In some cars the engine turns the front wheels. This is called front-wheel drive.

4. The propeller shaft turns the axle and this turns the back wheels.

1. Turning the key starts the engine.

2. Petrol in the engine is mixed with air. Electric sparks make the mixture explode over and over again, pushing pistons up and down.

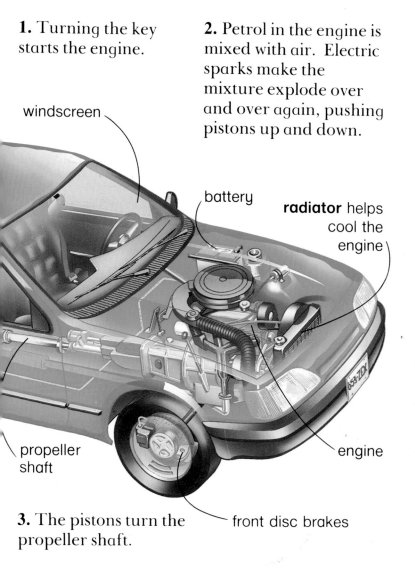

windscreen

battery

radiator helps cool the engine

propeller shaft

engine

3. The pistons turn the propeller shaft.

front disc brakes

Big cars, small cars

Cars come in many shapes and sizes. People use them for all kinds of different jobs.

This car has big wheels for driving across rough ground.

Cars with powerful engines can tow heavy loads.

A sports car has a long, low shape. This helps it go fast.

An estate car has lots of room to store luggage in. A roof rack can be useful too.

Taxis carry people around towns and cities.

A small car is easier to park in a busy street than a big car.

Motoring then and now

When cars were first invented, motoring was a real adventure. The cars often broke down and there were no proper roads. People wore goggles to keep dust out of their eyes and coats to keep them warm.

Motoring is very different today. Modern cars are fast and comfortable and roads and motorways criss-cross the countryside. But there are so many cars that they cause traffic jams and pollute the air with their exhausts.

At the garage

Like all machines, cars need looking after.

Without petrol the car will not go. The oil in the engine should be checked regularly. The air pressure in the tyres should also be checked from time to time. Keeping a car clean helps protect it against rust.

At the garage, mechanics service and repair cars. They check the engine, brakes and other parts and replace them if they have worn out. They can raise the car on a ramp to work underneath it.

Racing cars

Racing cars are built to go much faster than ordinary cars. During a race, they can reach speeds of nearly 400 kilometres an hour. Air rushing over the aerofoils at the front and back of the car pushes the car downwards to help keep the wheels on the track.

If the weather is dry, racing cars use tyres called slicks. These have no tread, or pattern, cut in them. If the race track is wet, they use treaded tyres, which give a better grip on the track.

Buses and coaches

The first buses were pulled by horses. Later there were buses on rails, called trams. Today most buses have diesel-oil engines.

This brightly coloured bus is used in Pakistan. When the bus is full, people sit on the roof.

This London double-decker bus can carry more than 70 people.

A trolley bus runs on electricity.
It picks up electricity from
overhead wires.

An articulated bus is
extra long. The bus
can bend at the join
to go round corners.

Coaches take people
on long-distance
journeys.

An articulated truck

trailer carries the load

trailer hook fits into the fifth wheel to link the trailer and the tractor unit

fifth wheel

diesel oil for the engine is carried in the **fuel tank**

An articulated truck is made up of two parts: a trailer and a tractor unit. The trailer is like a big container. It has no engine and is pulled along by the tractor unit. Because an articulated truck is made up of two parts, it can go round tight corners.

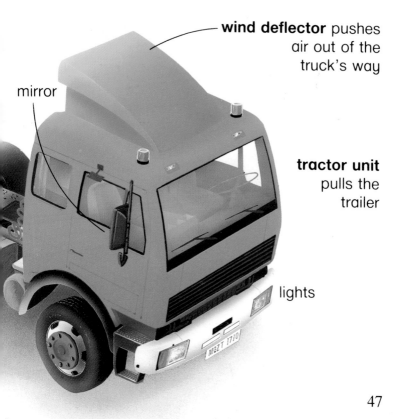

wind deflector pushes air out of the truck's way

mirror

tractor unit pulls the trailer

lights

47

The truck driver

At a busy warehouse, a forklift truck loads the trailer. Once everything is in place, the driver can set off. On a long trip, he may be away from home for a week or more.

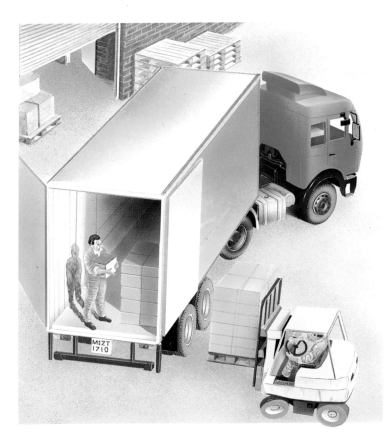

A truck driver keeps in touch with other
drivers using a telephone in the cab. A jack
comes in useful if he has to change a wheel.
After a hard day's driving, the driver climbs
into his bunk bed at the back of the cab. At
the end of the journey, he hands over his
delivery papers and the trailer is unloaded.

Special trucks

Trucks are designed and built for the different jobs they do.

A tanker carries petrol, gas or chemicals inside a strong metal tank.

The trailer of a refrigerated truck is cold inside, like a fridge or freezer, so that it can keep food fresh.

A car transporter carries new cars from the factory to the showroom.

This logging truck has a crane to lift logs on to the trailer.

A roadtrain is a truck that pulls three or more trailers. It is used on very long journeys.

Emergency!

Fire! Cars and cyclists make way for the emergency vehicles as they speed through the streets. Firemen are soon at work putting out the fire. Policemen keep people away from the danger area. The ambulance arrives in case anyone is hurt.

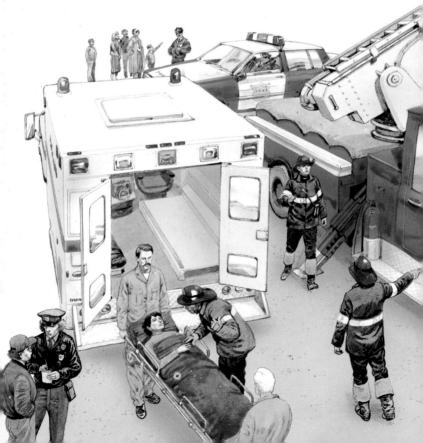

The farm tractor has a powerful engine and big back wheels. The deep tread, or pattern, on the tyres helps them grip the mud when the tractor is pulling a heavy plough up and down a field.

The big tyres on this all-terrain vehicle help it travel over rough ground. It can climb steep hills and splash through mud and water. To steer, the driver uses handlebars instead of a steering wheel.

A mobile crane

The mobile crane can travel on roads like any truck. But at the building site, it puts down metal legs, called stabilizers, that raise it off the ground and keep it steady as it lifts its heavy load.

Pulley wheels wind the load up and down on wires.

The driver pulls levers inside the cab to work the crane's arm, or boom.

stabilizers

The boom can be made longer or shorter, like a telescope.

boom

H376 DNK

57

Building a road

First, planners make maps to show where the new road will go. They work out how much traffic will use the road. Then, huge machines get to work building the road.

1. Bulldozers clear away piles of rocks and earth.

2. Machines called scrapers level the ground to make it flat.

dumper truck

3. Dumper trucks carry away the waste soil and deliver a mixture of crushed stones called hardcore. This is pressed into the earth to make a firm base for the road. Graders then smooth the surface of the road ready for the top layer.

roller

4. A paving machine spreads a layer of tarmac on the road. Tarmac is a mixture of small stones and tar. Finally, a roller presses the tarmac down to make it smooth and hard.

bulldozer

scraper

grader

paving machine

59

Bridges and tunnels

Bridges and tunnels shorten journeys.
A bridge can carry railway tracks across a
river, or take cars safely over another road.
Tunnels allow us to go through mountains,
beneath city streets and under rivers.

To build a tunnel, engineers must bore through rock under the ground. If the rock is hard, machines drill holes for explosives that will blast the rock away.

If the rock is softer, a machine called a tunnel-boring machine is used. This has a cutting face that bites away the rock. The tunnel is then lined with steel and concrete.

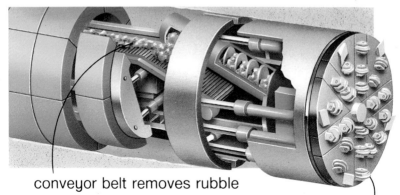

conveyor belt removes rubble

cutting face

Amazing facts

There are more than 500 million cars in the world. About one third of them are driven in North America.

The biggest land vehicles are two giant crawlers used to carry space rockets to the launch pad at Cape Canaveral in the United States of America. Each is as big as a twelve-storey building.

The world's fastest passenger car is the Jaguar XJ220. It can go at over 340 kilometres an hour.

The fastest land vehicle in the world is *Thrust 2*. This car has jet engines and can travel at over 1,019 kilometres an hour.

The Saint Gotthard Tunnel is the world's longest road tunnel. It is 16 kilometres long and burrows beneath the Alps in Switzerland.

Wheels

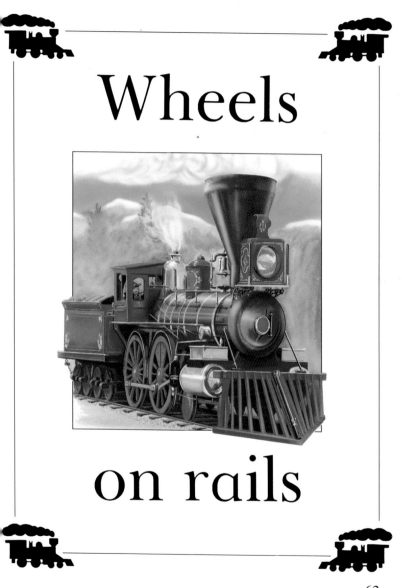

on rails

At the station

Trains start and end their journeys at stations.
Stations are busy places, with people
hurrying to catch their trains. Indicator
boards show passengers which platform to
go to and what time the train will depart.

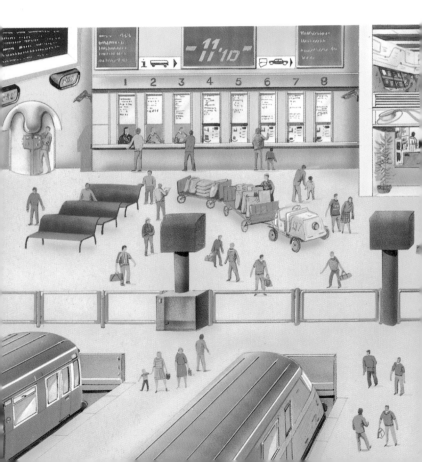

Trains come and go all day long. A fast express train may be taking passengers to a city hundreds of kilometres away. Slower trains bring people to work in the city. Trains carry letters and parcels too.

A high-speed train

This French TGV is the world's quickest passenger train. (In French, TGV stands for High-Speed Train.) The TGV travels at speeds of up to 300 kilometres an hour. Its streamlined shape helps it to go fast.

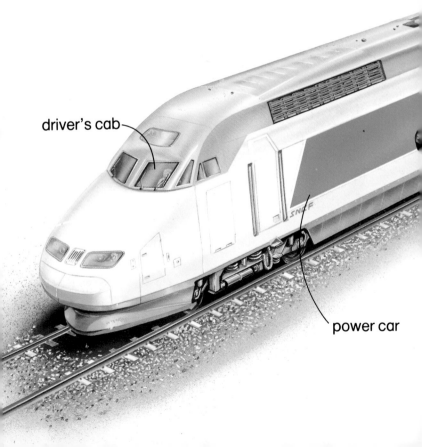

driver's cab

power car

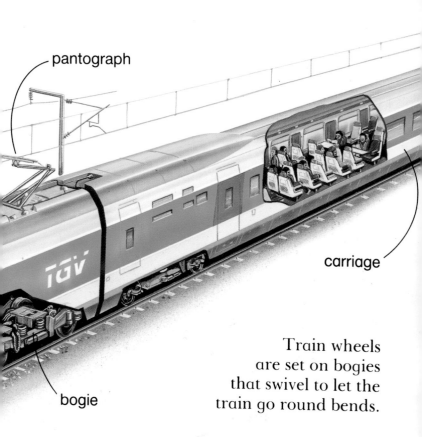

pantograph

carriage

bogie

Train wheels are set on bogies that swivel to let the train go round bends.

The TGV is powered by electricity. It picks up electricity from an overhead wire with a sliding arm called a pantograph. Motors in the power cars use this electricity to drive the wheels and pull the carriages along.

Driving a train

Inside the driver's cab on a TGV there is a computer that tells the driver how fast he can go and when to slow down and stop. The driver controls the speed of the train with the wheel in front of him.

Train wheels have no tyres. Instead they have a rim to stop them slipping off the rail. If a train wants to turn left or right, it must move on to a different track. Movable tracks, called points, switch the train from one track to another. The points are controlled electronically from a signal box.

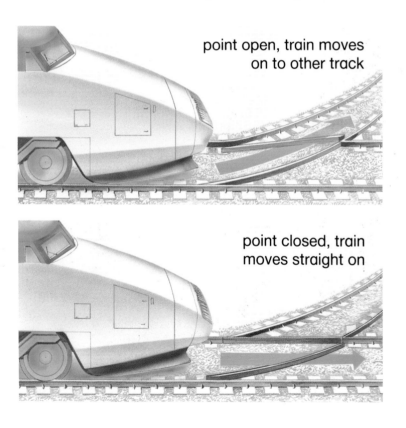

point open, train moves on to other track

point closed, train moves straight on

A steam train

Steam trains burn wood and coal to heat water and make steam. The steam then pushes pistons that turn the wheels.

This steam train travelled across North America over 100 years ago. The cowcatcher in front cleared the track.

🚂 Trains around the world

Steam trains are still used on some railways. This one is in India.

A modern diesel train burns oil to make electricity. The electricity drives the train's motors.

A rack and pinion train is designed to climb steep hills. It has an extra wheel with teeth that fit into notches on a third rail. This stops the train slipping down the hill.

third rail

🚂 Underground

Underground trains carry people through tunnels under busy city streets. The trains run on electric power. Passengers go down in lifts or on escalators to reach the platforms.

Like a train that runs underground, a hanging monorail can save space in a busy city. Monorail means the train travels on just one rail. A hanging monorail, such as the one shown above, hangs below the rail. A sturdy arm holds it in place. Other monorails sit on the rail.

Freight trains

As well as carrying passengers, trains also transport all kinds of goods, called freight, from one city to another.

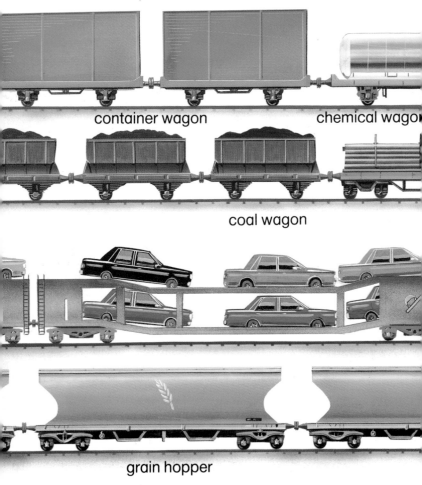

container wagon

chemical wagon

coal wagon

grain hopper

Freight trains can be made up of as many as 150 different wagons. They are linked together in a freight yard.

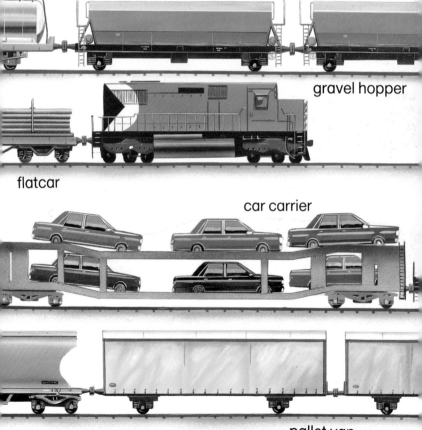

gravel hopper

flatcar

car carrier

pallet van

Amazing facts

The first public steam railway was the Stockton and Darlington Railway, in England. In 1825 a train made up of 33 carriages carried the first passengers at a top speed of 24 kilometres an hour.

The first underground railway opened in London in 1863. To begin with, the trains were pulled by steam locomotives, so the tunnels were always full of smoke.

The speed record for a train is 515 kilometres an hour. This was set by a French TGV in 1990. New trains that are being developed, called Maglev trains, could go even faster. Maglev trains float above the track and are pushed along by magnets.

The longest railway in the world is over 9,400 kilometres long and runs from Moscow to Nakhodka, in Russia.

Ocean

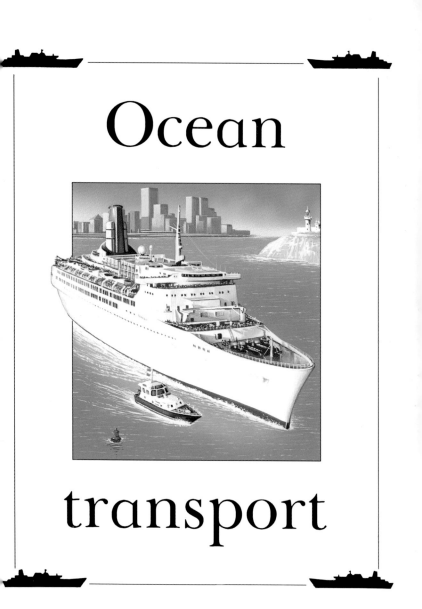

transport

 # A port

At a port, ships are loaded and unloaded.
Tugs guide big ships to their parking places,
called berths. Huge cranes lift cargo off the
ships to be stored in warehouses. To keep
the water deep, dredgers scoop up mud
from the bottom.

ferry

warehouse

dredger

tug

crane

An ocean liner

An ocean liner is like a floating hotel. The passengers enjoy their journey in comfort. They can swim, play games on deck, or watch a film while the crew run the ship.

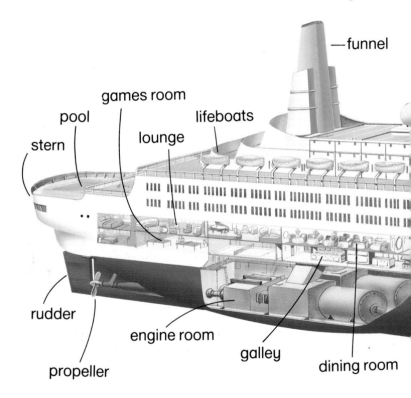

funnel

games room

pool

lifeboats

lounge

stern

rudder

engine room

galley

propeller

dining room

The parts of a ship all have names. The body is called the hull. The front is called the bow and the back is called the stern. Bedrooms are called cabins and the kitchen is called the galley. The captain controls the ship from the bridge.

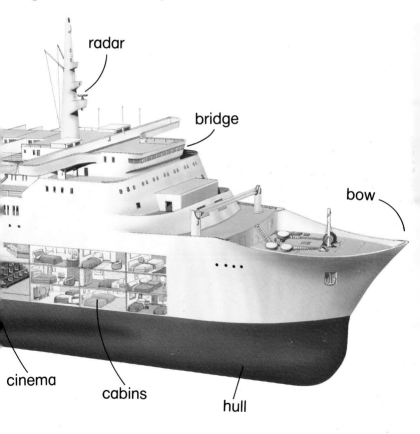

radar

bridge

bow

cinema

cabins

hull

Navigation

lighthouse

buoy

buoy

Taking a liner in and out of port can be difficult. Usually, a pilot who knows the port well takes control of the ship. Floating buoys show the pilot where the channels of deep water are. The flashing light on a lighthouse warns ships of dangerous rocks.

Navigation means finding the way. Once the ship is out on the open sea, the captain and crew on the bridge work out the ship's course using maps. They use radar to spot other ships, and satellite signals to check their position.

The engine room

Down in the hull are the ship's engines. Some ships have diesel engines, others have gas turbine engines. The engines turn the propeller and this drives the ship through the water. The rudder steers the ship.

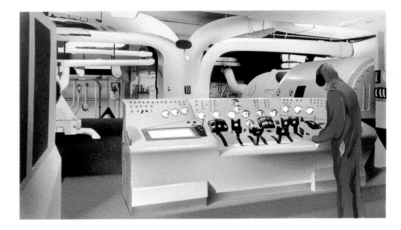

rudder

propeller

How a ship floats

The weight of a ship's hull pushes it down into the water. But the water tries to get back and pushes up against the hull. If the two pushes are equal, the ship floats. But if the ship is made too heavy, it will sink.

Marks on the ship's side, called the Plimsoll line, show how low down in the water the ship can safely go.

The weight of the ship pushes it down.

The water pushes up against the hull.

All kinds of ships

Ships come in different shapes and sizes.

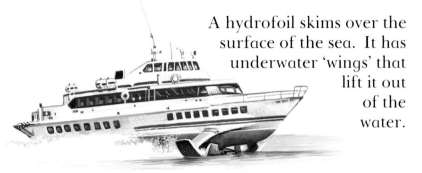

A hydrofoil skims over the surface of the sea. It has underwater 'wings' that lift it out of the water.

Hovercraft float on a cushion of air. Fans blow air downwards and lift the hovercraft off the water.

Paddle steamers travel up and down rivers. They are driven by a big wheel at the stern.

Lifeboats rescue people at sea. They are small, but they are almost unsinkable.

Fishing trawlers have a winding engine at the stern to haul in their heavy nets.

Supertankers carry oil in huge tanks. They are the biggest ships in the world.

87

 # Canals

Canals are waterways built by people.
When a canal runs through land that is on a
slope, it must be built in a series of steps. To
move up and down these steps, canal boats
have to go through locks.

This canal boat is going up a step. Once the boat is in the lock, the gates are closed. Then water is slowly let into the lock. When the water has risen to the correct level, the gates open and the canal boat moves on.

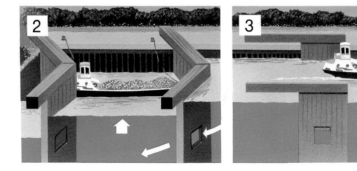

Sailing ships

Sailing ships are powered by the wind pushing against the sails. Sailing ships like this one carried people and cargo over 100 years ago. But people stopped using big sailing ships when faster steamships were invented.

The junk is
a Chinese
sailing ship.

This racing yacht can go very
fast. The big sail at the front is
called a spinnaker.

A catamaran has two
hulls. Most sailing
boats have only one.

A submarine

The rudder and hydroplanes steer the submarine under water.

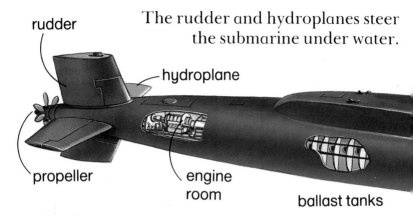

rudder

hydroplane

propeller

engine room

ballast tanks

Submarines are ships that go under water. They can stay under water for weeks without coming to the surface. The commander controls the submarine from the control room. By raising the periscope, he can look around above the water.

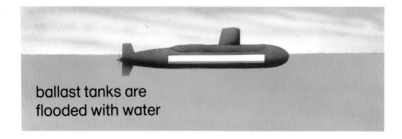

ballast tanks are flooded with water

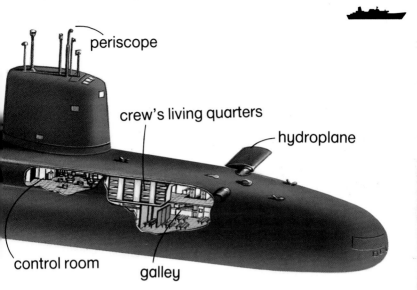

periscope

crew's living quarters

hydroplane

control room

galley

To dive, the submarine's ballast tanks are flooded with seawater. The submarine sinks. To come back up to the surface, air is blown into the ballast tanks, pushing out the water.

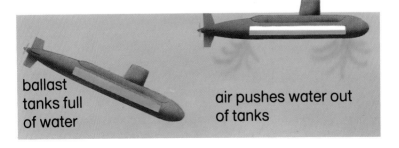

ballast tanks full of water

air pushes water out of tanks

Amazing facts

The first expedition to sail around the world was led by the explorer Ferdinand Magellan in 1519. The voyage took nearly three years and proved that the Earth is round, and not flat as many people had believed.

Over a hundred years ago, the fastest sailing ships were clipper ships. A clipper could cross the Atlantic in 12 days. The fastest crossing by a modern passenger liner is three and a half days.

The world's biggest ship is an oil tanker, *Hellas Fos*, of 555,051 tonnes. The largest passenger ship is the cruise liner *Norway*, which is 315 metres long.

Famous shipwrecks include the English warship *Mary Rose* and the liner *Titanic*. The *Mary Rose* sank when it turned over in 1545, and the *Titanic* hit an iceberg in 1912.

Into

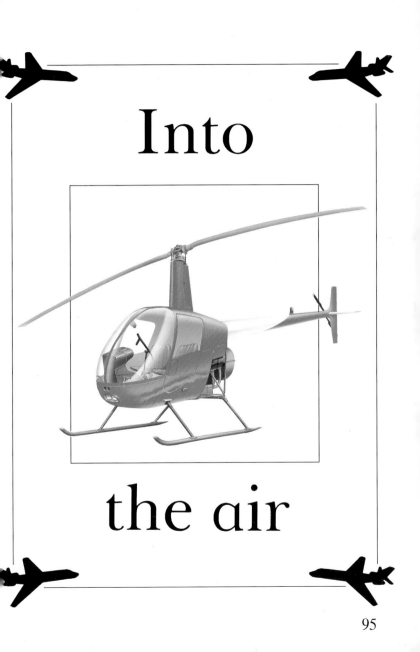

the air

✈ At the airport

An airport needs lots of space. There are long runways, hangars for aircraft that need servicing and repairs, and terminal buildings where the passengers check in.

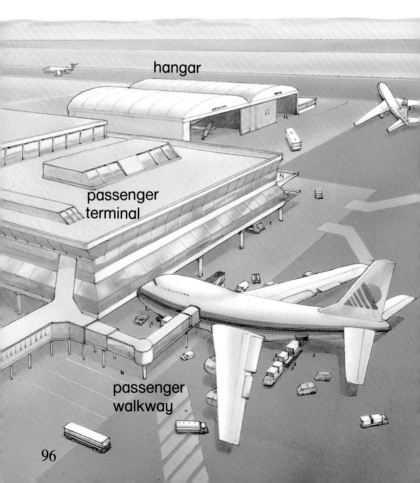

hangar

passenger terminal

passenger walkway

Before the passengers board their plane, it must be cleaned and refuelled. Food is taken on board and the baggage is stored in the hold. When everything is ready, the plane moves to the end of the runway to wait for permission to take off.

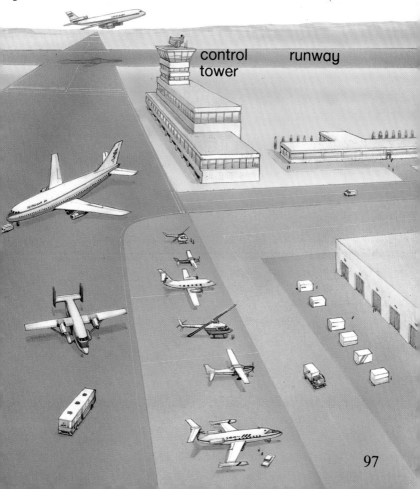

control tower

runway

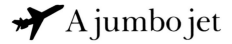 A jumbo jet

This Boeing 747 is the world's biggest passenger plane. It has room for about 400 passengers. Its four turbofan engines push it through the air at over 900 kilometres an hour. It has a wide body, called the fuselage, thin strong wings and a big tailfin.

moving the **ailerons** makes the plane roll sideways

top deck

flight deck

radar in the nose helps guide the pilot through the skies

galley

nose wheels

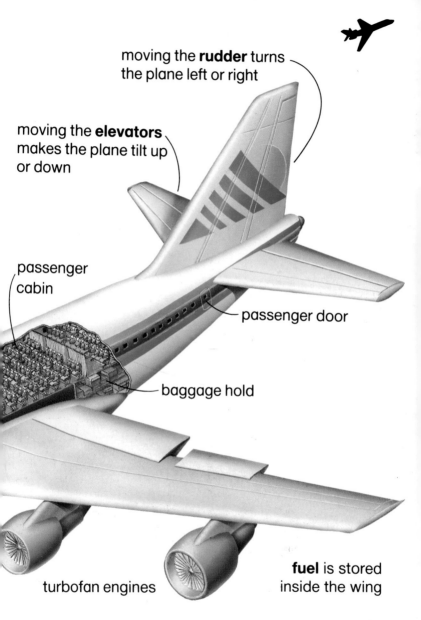

moving the **rudder** turns the plane left or right

moving the **elevators** makes the plane tilt up or down

passenger cabin

passenger door

baggage hold

turbofan engines

fuel is stored inside the wing

99

✈ Catching a plane

When passengers arrive at the airport, they check their baggage in at the airline desk. If they are travelling abroad, they must then go through passport control.

loading the plane

While passengers wait to board the plane, baggage handlers load their baggage into the plane's hold. During the flight, the cabin crew look after the passengers. They serve drinks and meals. Once the plane has landed, the passengers collect their baggage.

unloading the plane

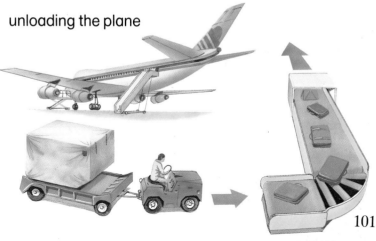

✈ Permission to take off

The pilot waits for the controllers in the control tower to give him permission to take off. The controllers use radar to keep track of all the planes in the air or on the ground.

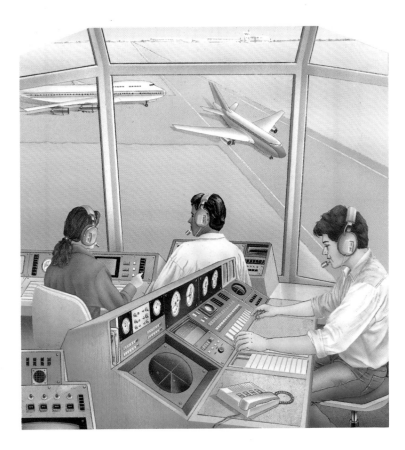

Computers on the flight deck help the pilot control the plane. They show him how high the plane is flying and how fast it is going. Even if the computers break down, the pilot can still fly the plane using instruments such as the altimeter and the artificial horizon.

altimeter

artificial horizon

✈ How a plane flies

As the engines drive the plane along the runway, air flows around the wings. The faster the plane goes, the faster the air flows.

The forward push that comes from the engines is called thrust.

The upward push is called lift.

Air flowing over and under the curved wings creates lift.

The wings of a plane have a curved shape. When air flows over and under the wings, it creates an upward push on the plane. As the plane picks up speed, the upward push gets stronger. When it is strong enough, it lifts the plane off the ground.

Drag slows the plane down.

The weight of the plane pulls it downwards.

✈ All kinds of aircraft

Any flying machine is an aircraft. Aircraft
can be huge or tiny. Some can fly faster
than others, but each has a job to do.

A glider does not have
an engine. It glides on
currents of air.

An ultra-light is a tiny
one-person plane.

This plane can scoop up
water from lakes and
use it to put out
a forest fire.

Concorde is the only supersonic
airliner in the world. It is
supersonic because it can
fly faster than the
speed of sound.

This small commuter jet
carries people on
business trips.

The Super Guppy looks like a flying whale.
It was built to carry the parts of other aircraft
and rockets.

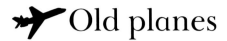Old planes

The first pilots were brave and skilful. Their planes were small and slow, but they made history in the air.

Orville and Wilbur Wright flew the first real aeroplane in 1903.

In 1909 Louis Blériot was the first person to fly across the sea from France to England.

In 1927 Charles Lindbergh was the first pilot to fly across the Atlantic Ocean alone.

✈ Military planes

Air forces and navies use special planes.
Some are very fast fighters and bombers.
Some, such as the Harrier jump jet, do not
need a long runway. They can land in a
field or on the deck of a ship.

Hornet

Mirage

Harrier

Helicopters

A helicopter has spinning rotor blades instead of wings. It can fly upwards or downwards or sideways and can even hover in mid-air.

To move the helicopter in all these different directions, the pilot changes the angle of the rotor blades using a joy stick and foot pedals.

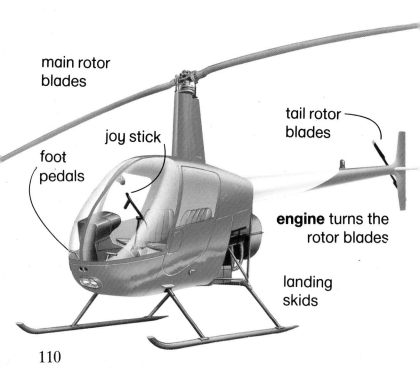

main rotor
blades

joy stick

foot
pedals

tail rotor
blades

engine turns the
rotor blades

landing
skids

Helicopters are often used to rescue people at sea. The pilot keeps the helicopter steady while one of the crew is lowered on a line to help the person in the water. Then both can be winched up to safety.

Amazing facts

In 1933 Wiley Post was the first person to fly solo around the world. His journey was 25,000 kilometres long and took him 7 days, 18 hours and 49 minutes.

In 1986 a plane flew non-stop around the world without refuelling. Two pilots were squashed inside the small cabin for 9 days, 3 minutes and 44 seconds.

The world's heaviest aircraft is the Russian An-225 Dream. It weighs 508 tonnes.

The fastest aircraft of all time was the American X-15A-2, a rocket plane that reached 7,274 kilometres an hour in 1967.

The Harrier jump jet is a V/STOL plane. This means that it can fly straight up or down. The letters V/STOL stand for Vertical/Short Take Off and Landing.

The

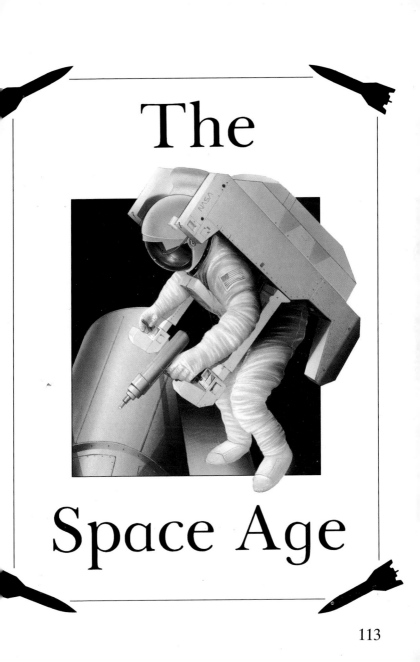

Space Age

 # Lift off

It takes five engines, burning 20 tonnes of fuel a second, to lift the space shuttle off the launch pad. The shuttle can carry up to seven astronauts into Space. It can also carry satellites and a laboratory in its large payload bay.

main fuel tank

payload bay

booster rockets give extra power during launch

About two minutes after lift off, the two booster rockets fall away from the shuttle and parachute into the sea.

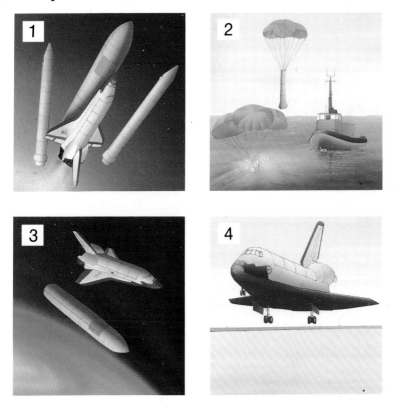

A few minutes later, the main fuel tank also falls away. Once its mission is over, the shuttle returns to Earth and lands on a runway like an aeroplane.

On board the shuttle

The living area and the flight deck are in the nose of the shuttle. In the middle is the payload bay. Once the shuttle is out in Space, the doors of the payload bay can open. On this mission the shuttle is carrying a telescope and a spacelab.

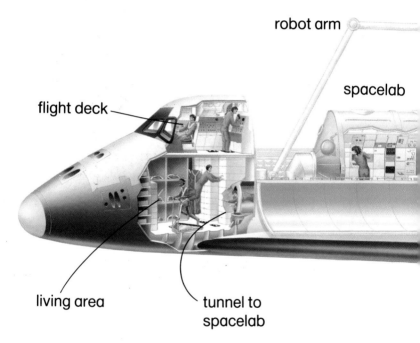

robot arm

spacelab

flight deck

living area

tunnel to spacelab

The astronauts carry out scientific experiments in the lab. One of the astronauts is working out in the payload bay. He is attached to a robot arm to stop him floating away.

main engines

telescope

small **thruster rockets** move the shuttle while it is in Space

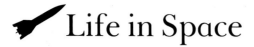 Life in Space

In Space there is no gravity. So unless they are strapped down, the astronauts float about inside the shuttle. They even have to strap themselves on to the exercise machine and into their sleeping bags.

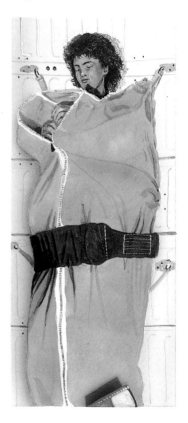

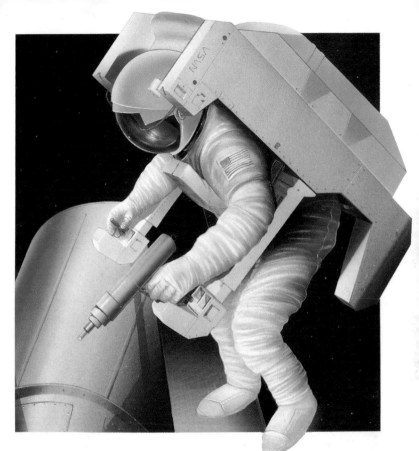

Because there is no air in
Space, astronauts must wear a spacesuit
when they are working outside the shuttle.
This astronaut is also wearing an MMU –
a Man Manoeuvering Unit. By firing jets in
the MMU, the astronaut can move about.

Amazing facts

The Space Age began in 1957 when the USSR launched the first artificial satellite. It was called *Sputnik 1*.

The world's first human space traveller was Yuri Gagarin of the USSR. He travelled once around the Earth in 1961.

The first people to land on the Moon were the American astronauts Neil Armstrong and Edwin Aldrin. They landed in the *Apollo 11* spacecraft on 21 July, 1969.

In 1977 the Americans launched the *Voyager 2* robot spacecraft on a voyage of exploration. It sent back television pictures of four planets – Jupiter, Saturn, Uranus and Neptune – and is still travelling out in Space.

INDEX

The editor would like to thank Trans World Airlines Inc. and the many other companies and individuals who assisted in the preparation of this book.

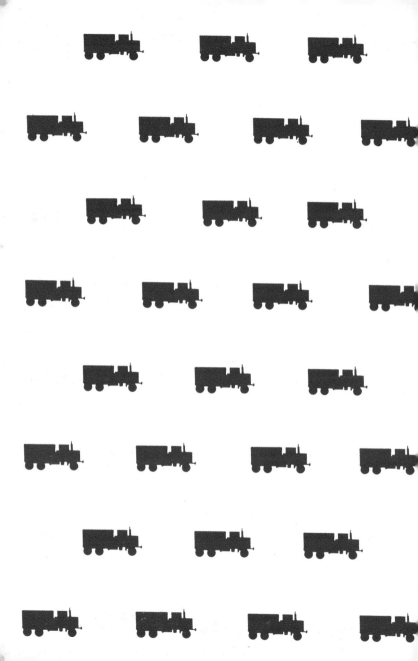